D1707521

DISCOVER
ANCIENT
EGYPT

Bramwell, Neil D., 1932
Discover ancient Egypt
2014.
33305230934014
ca   12/01/14

ILIZATIONS

DISCOVER ANCIENT EGYPT

Neil D. Bramwell

Enslow Publishers, Inc.
40 Industrial Road
Box 398
Berkeley Heights, NJ 07922
USA
http://www.enslow.com

ANCIENT EGYPT

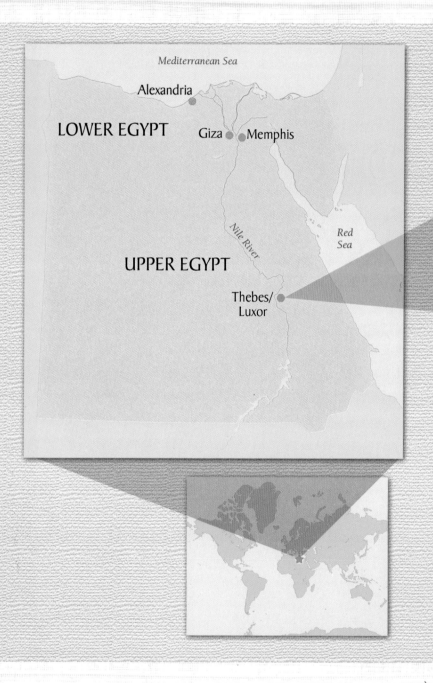

Valley of the Kings

■ Temple of Hatshepsut

Valley of
the Queens

■ Temple of
Ramses II

■ Karnak Temple

THEBES

Copyright © 2014 by Enslow Publishers, Inc.

All rights reserved.

No part of this book may be reproduced by any means without the written permission of the publisher.

Originally published as *Ancient Egypt* in 2004.

Library of Congress Cataloging-in-Publication Data

Bramwell, Neil D., 1932–

    Discover ancient Egypt / Neil D. Bramwell.

      p. cm. — (Discover ancient civilizations)

    Summary: "Learn about the art and cultural contributions, family life, religions and people of ancient Egypt"—Provided by publisher.

    Includes bibliographical references and index.

    ISBN 978-0-7660-4195-0

    1. Egypt—Civilization—To 332 B.C.—Juvenile literature. 2. Egypt—History—To 332 B.C.—Juvenile literature. I. Title. II. Series: Discover ancient civilizations.

    DT61.B67835 2014

    932—dc23

                                      2012011571

Future editions:

Paperback ISBN 978-1-4644-0333-0

ePUB ISBN 978-1-4645-1186-8

Single-User PDF ISBN 978-1-4646-1186-5

Multi-User PDF ISBN 978-0-7660-5815-0

Printed in the United States of America

102013 Lake Book Manufacturing, Inc., Melrose Park, IL

10 9 8 7 6 5 4 3 2 1

To Our Readers: We have done our best to make sure all Internet Addresses in this book were active and appropriate when we went to press. However, the author and the publisher have no control over and assume no liability for the material available on those Internet sites or on other Web sites they may link to. Any comments or suggestions can be sent by e-mail to comments@enslow.com or to the address on the back cover.

Every effort has been made to locate all copyright holders of material used in this book. If any errors or omissions have occurred, corrections will be made in future editions of this book.

♻ Enslow Publishers, Inc., is committed to printing our books on recycled paper. The paper in every book contains 10% to 30% post-consumer waste (PCW). The cover board on the outside of each book contains 100% PCW. Our goal is to do our part to help young people and the environment too!

Illustrations Credits: ©2012 Photos.com, a division of Getty Images. All rights reserved., pp. 5(left, center); 24, 26, 32, 58, 59, 60-61, 80, 88-89; ©Clipart.com/ © 2012 Photos.com, a division of Getty Images. All rights reserved., pp. 16, 25, 35; ©Corel Corporation, pp. 5(right), 14-15, 41, 44-45, 47, 48, 50, 57, 62, 66-67, 78; ©Enslow Publishers, Inc., p. 21; Amanda Lewis/© 2011 Photos.com, a division of Getty Images. All rights reserved., p. 73; Kristin McCarthy/© Enslow Publishers, Inc., pp. 4-5, 28; Mikhail Dudarev/iStockphoto/©Thinkstock, pp. 70-71; Prill Mediendesign/iStockphoto/ Thinkstock, p. 12; Shutterstock, pp. 83, 90.

Cover Credits: Background: Mikhail Dudarev/iStockphoto/©Thinkstock; Foreground: Prill Mediendesign/iStockphoto/Thinkstock.

Table of CONTENTS

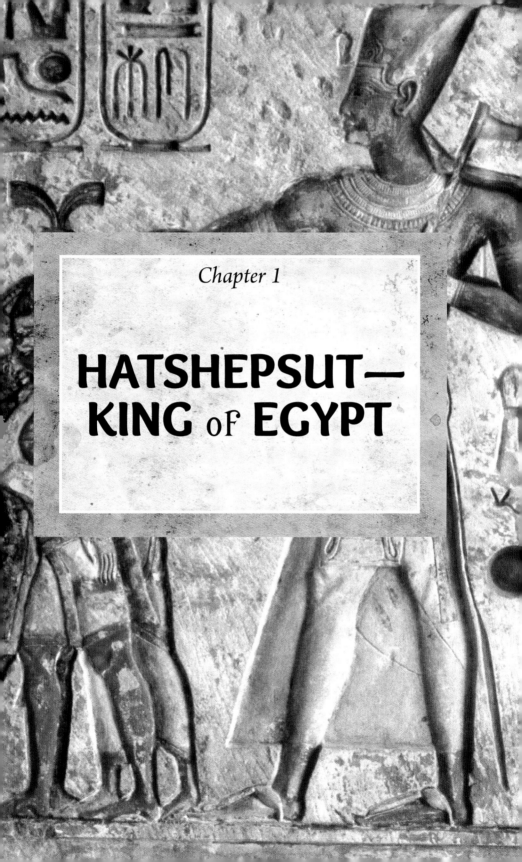

Chapter 1

HATSHEPSUT— KING OF EGYPT

On one of the temple walls at Thebes, Hatshepsut, king of Egypt, commissioned a scene depicting her birth as a divine child. It was her way of establishing her claim to rule as king. Hatshepsut was a woman and could have ruled Egypt as its queen. There had been ruling queens of Egypt before and after Hatshepsut but queens could not exercise all the powers of a king, particularly those of High Priest of Egypt, and Hatshepsut was determined to rule with *all* the powers of the king.

Hatshepsut's Regency

Thutmose III became pharaoh, or king, of Egypt around 1479 B.C., on the death of Thutmose II, his father and Hatshepsut's husband. Thutmose III, Hatshepsut's stepson, was a young child at the time, so Hatshepsut was made regent—one who governs until a child becomes old enough to rule.

But Hatshepsut wasn't content with the limited power that regents had, and by the seventh year of the regency (1473 B.C.), she had become powerful enough to declare herself king of Egypt.[1]

A female king was rare in Egyptian history. Of the many kings, only four are known to have been women.[2] Hatshepsut ruled with all the power of a male king. To fortify her image as king, Hatshepsut wore the official dress of a male pharaoh when performing official duties. Images of her found on the temples and monuments show this. For Hatshepsut, the official male dress, which consisted of a short kilt, the male headdress, and at times, even a false beard, symbolized the male king's absolute power. Hatshepsuet was not pretending to be a man, though. Statues and other images of her show her with the body of a female.[3]

Hatshepsut is shown at her temple at
Deir el-Bahri in this row of Osiris statues.
The Egyptians believed that the Pharaoh
became Osiris when he died.

Co-ruler

Hatshepsut did not remove Thutmose III from the throne. Officially, she ruled as co-king, but Hatshepsut exercised sole power for about twenty years. During her rule, Egypt was for the most part at peace, except for at least one military campaign in Nubia (modern-day Sudan), on Egypt's southern border, at which Hatshepsut may have been present.[4] She also sent an expedition to Punt, a land believed to have been located near the Eritrean coast on the Red Sea. The expedition returned with such wonderful products that Hatshepsut had the event recorded on one of the walls in her temple at Deir el-Bahri.[5]

Deir el-Bahri

Throughout her reign, Hatshepsut built and restored numerous temples and monuments. One of the world's most beautiful buildings commissioned by

Hathshepsut's Temple in Deir el-Bahri is one of many structures erected by this pharaoh.

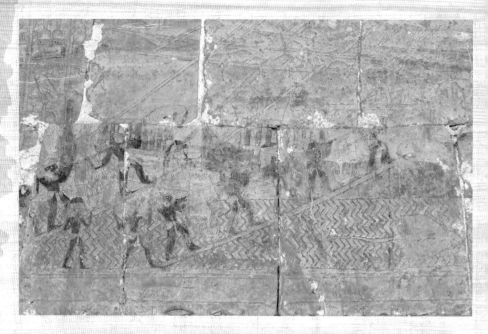

Bas-relief on the walls of Hatshepsut's temple showing the results of the trade mission to the land of Punt. Egyptians can be seen loading their ships with young sandalwood trees and other goods.

Hatshepsut is Deir el-Bahri. Chapels for Hatshepsut and her father, Thutmose I, were built as part of this temple. It was here that she had inscribed a scene showing her father declaring Hatshepsut his successor as king.[6] She used this fantasy as propaganda to support her position.

Some years after Hatshepsut's death, her successor, Thutmose III, deliberately destroyed images and other records of Hatshepsut as king.

About the twentieth year of her reign as king, Hatshepsut disappears from the Egyptian record. Nothing is known of her death. Thutmose III asserted his right to rule and did so for another thirty-two years as one of Egypt's most powerful kings and military leaders.[7]

In the last years of Thutmose III's rule, a deliberate campaign was conducted throughout Egypt to destroy all statues and pictures of Hatshepsut in an attempt to erase memory of her reign. Historians at first believed hatred of Hatshepsut's rule was the cause of the destruction. Now, politics, not hatred, is thought to have been the motive.

Thousands of years later, the discoveries of the magnificent temple of Deir el-Bahri and the tomb Hatshepsut commissioned to be built in the Valley of the Kings have once again brought King Hatshepsut to life.

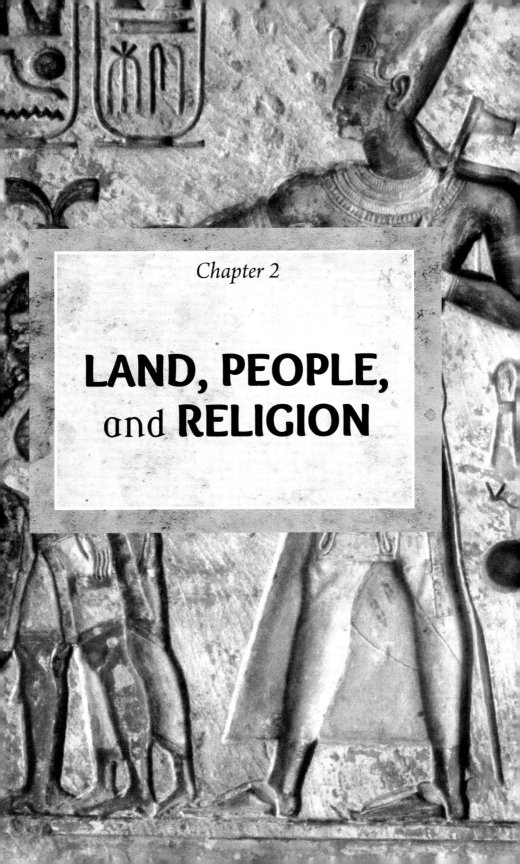

Chapter 2

LAND, PEOPLE, and RELIGION

Through the years, the lands of ancient Egypt varied in size and name. The region of southern Egypt from the First Cataract, or waterfall, to Memphis, the first capital of unified Egypt, is called Upper Egypt. The region from Memphis to the Mediterranean Sea, which includes the area known as the "Delta," a broad triangular region, is called Lower Egypt. When unified, Upper and Lower Egypt were known as the "Two Lands."[1]

Ancient Egypt: A Time Line

Ancient Egypt's oldest civilization, thousands of years before Upper and Lower Egypt were united in 3100 B.C., is known as the Predynastic Period. Scholars often disagree on the exact dates for events in ancient Egypt. For example, some historians date the unification of Upper Egypt and Lower Egypt into one kingdom at 2850 B.C.[2]

The New Kingdom

■ New Kingdom under Thutmose I
┈ New Kingdom's northern border under Ramses II

Euphrates River

Aleppo

Mediterranean Sea

Delta

Jerusalem

CANAAN

Sinai Peninsula

Memphis

LOWER EGYPT

Nile River

Valley of the Kings

Thebes

UPPER EGYPT

Red Sea

NUBIA

A map of ancient Egypt during the New Kingdom (1550 B.C.—1080 B.C.)

Historians divide the history of ancient Egypt into three periods beginning with its unification. They are: the Old Kingdom (2686–2181 B.C.), the Middle Kingdom (2040–1730 B.C.), and the New Kingdom (1550–1080 B.C.). These kingdoms were periods in which the absolute rule of kings established a powerful central government. The periods between the kingdoms, when central government was weak, are known as Intermediate Periods. These periods are: the First Intermediate Period (2180–2040 B.C.), the Second Intermediate Period (1730–1550 B.C.), and the Third Intermediate Period (1080–664 B.C.).

Finally, there is the Late Period (664–332 B.C.). This period is divided by some into the Saite Period (664–525 B.C.), when a king from the city of Sais in the Delta ruled a unified Egypt, and the Late Period (525–332 B.C.), when the Persian Empire ruled Egypt.[3] Rule by the Greeks, under Alexander the Great, began in 332 B.C.

Nile River: Source of Greatness

The Nile River was key to the development of Egypt as a nation and to its ancient civilization. The Nile runs the entire length of Egypt from the First Cataract at the southern border of ancient Egypt, north to the Delta, where it divides into branches and finally empties into the Mediterranean Sea. The Nile was the only water source the Egyptians had. Each year in the fall, flooding of the Nile deposited a strip of immensely fertile soil about four to thirteen miles wide on both sides of the river.[4]

Deserts and Oases

To the east and west of the fertile land close to the Nile were vast deserts. The deserts of Egypt were not barren wastes, however, but were rich sources of gold and different types of stone, such as granite,

The Nile, the world's longest river, was ancient Egypt's lifeline, providing a desert land with its only source of water.

....

limestone, basalt, and alabaster. Stone were quarried from the deserts and mountains for the enormous building projects of the Egyptian kings.

In the desert to the west of Egypt were small isolated pockets of fertile land known as oases. These were linked by trade routes to Libya in the west and to Nubia along Egypt's southern border.[5]

Irrigation and Agriculture

Flooding of the Nile River was so efficient, not only at supplying rich soil but also in washing out the salts deposited over time, that little irrigation was required except for reclamation of the land, or restoring its usefulness. Irrigation consisted of building channels to divert the floodwaters, and dikes and riverbanks had to be maintained to contain them.

A shadoof or a counterbalanced sweep used since ancient times especially in Egypt for raising water to be used in irrigation.

Tomb painting of two noblemen hunting wild birds in the Nile marshes. Using a snake-shaped stick to knock down waterfowl, one man stands in a skiff made of papyrus. Hunting in ancient Egypt was not just a way of providing food. It also showed the hunter's courage and his dominance over animals.

A shadoof was the main irrigation device used by ancient Egyptians. It was a long pole mounted on a pivot. The pole had a weight on one end, and a bucket at the other. The bucket was dipped into the water, and the filled bucket was lifted and the water dumped onto the field.[6]

Farmers used wooden plows to produce crops of barley, wheat, vegetables, and flax, which was woven into linen by women.[7] Beer, made from barley, was an important part of the Egyptian diet. The swampy marshes provided safety and food for large numbers of waterfowl, such as ducks and geese, and provided an abundant source of papyrus reeds.

Papyrus had many uses in ancient Egypt. It was twisted into rope and woven to make baskets, mats for roofs, and window coverings. Papyrus was even used in making boats. However, its most important use was in the making of paper.[8]

Egyptian Gods and Goddesses

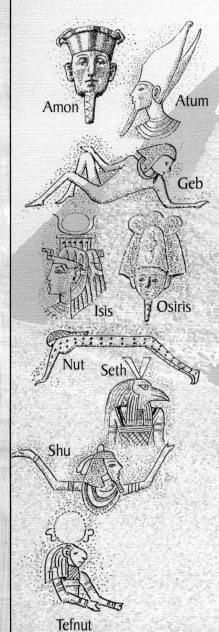

There were dozens of gods and goddesses that the ancient Egyptians worshipped. Below are some of the most important.

Amon—King of the Gods to those who lived in and around Thebes.

Anubis—God of mummification.

Atum—God of the setting sun.

Geb—God of the earth.

Hathor—Goddess of love, music, and women.

Horus—God of the sun and the pharaohs.

Isis—Goddess of magic.

Nut—Goddess of the sky.

Osiris—God of the afterlife.

Ra—Creator god of the sun.

Seth—God of storms and chaos.

Shu—God of the air.

Tefnut—Goddess of moisture and rain.

Thoth—God of wisdom and the moon.

Ancient Egypt's People

Early in their history, the Egyptians considered themselves one nationality sharing
the same beliefs and culture, but they also
recognized that they were made up of different groups. From the period of the
New Kingdom, the tomb of the king known
as Seti I contains a picture showing four
ethnic groups who made up the Egyptian
population: the remtu or native Egyptians,
Asiatics or Amu who lived to the east,
Nehesiu who lived to the south, and lastly
the Timihu who lived to the west. All had
different physical characteristics and wore
distinctive dress and headgear.[9]

Farmers and Craftsmen

The majority of the people in ancient Egypt
were farmers of small plots of land, but there
were also large numbers of skilled craftsmen
employed by the king. Their areas of special-
ilization included weaving, medicine, weapon

making, food preservation, construction, boat building, brick making, pottery, and working with gold.[10]

Priests

The priesthood formed a large group in ancient Egypt. During certain periods, both men and women served as priests, but most priests were men.[11] As noted earlier, King Hatshepsut assumed the role of high priest during her reign. Most of the priests worked part-time—one month a year. The priests were usually married, and, after serving in the temple, they returned to their families and occupations. Full-time priests wore special costumes.[12]

Religion in Ancient Egypt

An Egyptian belief held that in each human being there existed the Ka, the spiritual being of that human. The Ka continued its existence after death but required the preservation of its human body and daily offerings of food and drink.[13]

The Egyptians had many gods.[14] Every city and village in Egypt had its own special god to whom offerings were made. In many ancient Egyptian homes, images of the gods were placed on a small altar where daily prayers were offered.

Custom and the king's beliefs determined the formal worship and rituals of Egyptian religion. The king was thought to share the divinity of the gods. It was believed that at his death, the king lost his human form and became a god, equal to the other gods. The king's burial place contained a temple at which he was worshiped as a god and where daily offerings of food and drink were made to him.[15]

Despite changes in dynasties and rulers, including the rule of foreigners, the basic forms of religious beliefs and ceremonies of the ancient Egyptians did not change significantly until the coming of Christianity under the Roman Empire. However, changes

Bas-relif of Akhenaton (center) and his family adoring the light of the Aten (the sun disk). Akhenaton is best known in ancient Egyptian history for trying to change Egyptian worship from one of the multiple gods to the worship of a single god.

came during the time of Amenhotep IV
(1378–1352 B.C.) who attempted to intro-
duce a revolutionary change in Egypt's
religion and culture. He changed his name
from Amenhotep IV to Akhenaton, which
meant "He Who Is of Service to Aton."
Akhenaton sought to make Aton, the sun
god, the supreme god of Egypt. Worship of
the sun as the source of creation and all life
was not new in Egypt, but Akhenaton's
emphasis on the sole worship of Aton was.

Akhenaton closed many of the temples
devoted to other gods and confiscated
their property. Efforts to change the
religious beliefs of the Egyptians ended
with Akhenaton's death. It is not known
how Akhenaton died. His successor,
Tutankhamen, restored worship of the old
gods and their temples. Tutankhamen
described Akhenaton's rule as a mistake
that left Egypt in a wretched condition.[16]

Akhenaton's monuments and temples were destroyed and his name deleted from the official king lists.[17] Worship of the old gods was revived, and the capital city built at Akhenaton named "Akhetaton" (modern-day Tel el Amarna) fell into ruin.

Existence After Death

The ancient Egyptians believed in an afterlife, so preservation of the deceased body was considered essential for the continued existence of Ka, an individual's life-force. To preserve the body, the internal organs were removed and stored in special urns, known as canopic jars, and the body was treated with certain herbs. After drying, the body was wrapped in layers of cloth, often fine linen, into which jewels and magic inscriptions were placed. Some magic spells related to death and resurrection were repeated over the dead body. Such preserved bodies are popularly called mummies.

This wall painting is located in tomb of Sennutem and his wife. It shows the deceased man and his wife working in the "Fields of Content" or heaven. The Egyptians believed that the deceased spent much of their time there working in fertile fields.

Osiris, Isis, Horus, and Set

Four of the many gods worshipped by ancient Egyptians were Osiris, the god of the underworld and Egypt's first king; his sister and wife, Isis, the mother goddess; their son, Horus, god of the sky; and their brother, Set, god of wind and storms.

Many ancient Egyptians believed that Set, who was jealous of his brother Osiris, murdered him, cut up the body, and buried its parts in areas all over Egypt. (Egyptians believed that the Pharaoh became Osiris when he died.) Isis, after a long and difficult search, found the different parts of the body, reassembled them, and by magic restored Osiris to life. Horus, the son of Osiris and Isis, battled Set until Set recognized Horus as the king of mankind. The sun disk became the symbol for Horus and was placed on the doors of all the temples in Egypt. The story of the gods Osiris, Isis, Horus, and Set, with its themes of resurrection after death and the struggle of good against evil, was a strong element of Egyptian culture and religion throughout the ancient Egyptian history.

Pyramid and Coffin Texts

The scenes from the life of the king and hieroglyphic texts of rites and prayers—intended to transform the king at his death to a god—decorated the king's tomb. These texts, known as the Pyramid Texts, are first found in the pyramid of King Unas (2375–2345 B.C.). The texts include the story of Osiris and identify the king with Osiris. Equally important, the Pyramid Texts included formulas for the priests to recite to assist the dead in their travels to the afterlife.

Coffin Texts consist of inscriptions written inside coffins. These include magic formulas given for the dead to gather (in the afterlife) with family and friends.

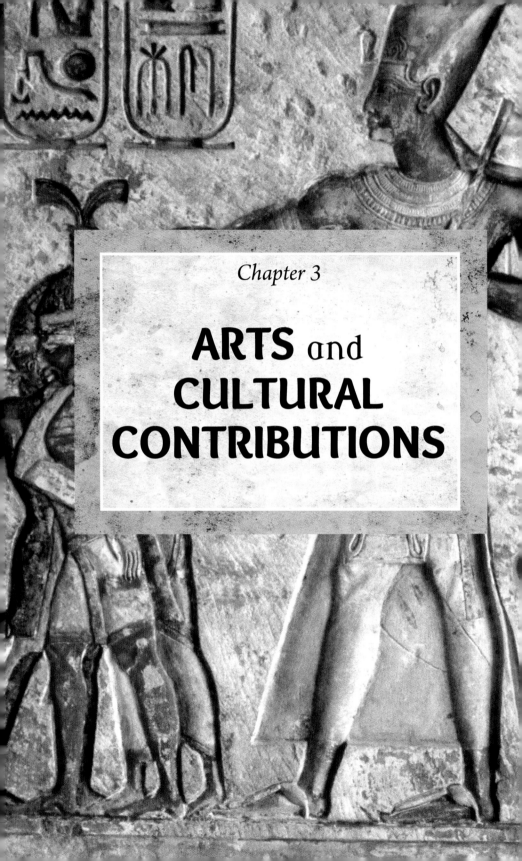

Chapter 3

ARTS and CULTURAL CONTRIBUTIONS

Arts and Cultural Contributions

The great pyramids, colossal statues, and huge temple complexes, particularly at Karnak and Luxor, are perhaps the most striking examples of Egyptian art. Equally as important as these monuments are Egyptian painting, sculpture, and the murals and bas-reliefs, a form of sculpture, that decorate the walls of the temples and tombs themselves. Beyond all of these, skilled goldsmiths left a treasure trove of jewels within the pyramids and temples.

Along with the beautiful designs, paintings, and sculptures that decorate Egypt's monuments, there are inscriptions. These inscriptions often describe events, memorialize a pharaoh's reign, or simply name the person depicted. They have given historians valuable information about the ancient Egyptian peoples.

Pyramids

Based on the Egyptians' belief in life after death, pyramids were built as tombs for the kings and queens. Around the pyramids were large complexes of temples and other buildings for priests and workers to carry out the daily services required for the king's existence in the afterlife.

There are many theories as to how the pyramids were built, including the use of ramps to allow the stones to be moved along as the pyramid rose, and pulleys and lifts to raise the massive blocks of stone. However, no solid evidence exists to show just how they were built.

The building of the pyramids is proof of the great power of the Egyptian king and the wealth and prosperity of Egypt in the Old Kingdom. Vast amounts of resources, manpower, and the skill to organize them were required to build these massive structures.[1]

The Step Pyramid

The first of the great pyramids is known as the Step Pyramid. It is believed to be the world's first complete stone building. The Step Pyramid is made of six gigantic platforms, placed one above the other, like a series of steps. It rises 204 feet above the ground. The substructure is a honeycomb of shafts and tunnels.

Egypt is known for its pyramids, including the Step Pyramid shown here. Completed about 2630 B.C., it is thought to be the world's first building made of stone rather than mud brick.

Imhotep built the Step Pyramid for King Djoser, the second king of the Third dynasty of the Old Kingdom. Imhotep, an official of the king, was not only a builder, but also a high priest, a scribe, and a man of great medical skill. In fact, he was later treated as a god and identified with the Greek god of healing.[2]

First True Pyramid and the Bent Pyramid

In 2613 B.C., Sneferu became king of Egypt and built as his tomb the first true pyramid. A true pyramid is a stone structure with a square base whose four sides are equal triangles that rise smoothly, inclining to a point above ground. Sneferu also built another pyramid, this one a bent pyramid whose sides abruptly change incline halfway up the pyramid.[3]

The Great Pyramid

The largest of the pyramids, the Great Pyramid, is the biggest stone building ever built. King Khufu, also known by the Greek name Cheops (2583–2560 B.C.), built the Great Pyramid. It contained nearly 6 million tons of stone and rose about 480 feet above the ground when it was built.[4]

Paintings and Reliefs

Egyptian paintings and bas-reliefs in the tombs were not intended for the public. They were to assist the dead in the afterlife. The painting of hunts, banquets, and family gatherings would help the dead repeat those events in the afterlife.[5] Even though these events were painted according to a rigid, stylized formula, they show the daily life of the ancient Egyptians in realistic detail.

The Great Pyramid was ordered to be built by King Khufu. Its entrance was used by the Egyptian builders who worked on the inside.

Paintings and bas-reliefs did not represent the insight of a single artist but were the result of many craftsmen operating under a highly organized system of rules and regulations. The style for depicting humans in Egyptian art developed as early as the Old Kingdom and continued in its basic form for about fifteen hundred years.[6]

Akhenaton's Contribution to Art

King Akhenaton attempted to make Egyptian painting depict the human form in more natural and significantly less formal poses. Akhenaton with his wife, Queen Nefertiti, and their children are often shown in affectionate, informal family scenes. Instead of being painted as a conquering hero, the king is shown as potbellied, with skinny arms and legs.[7] Following Akhenaton's death, this realism in art was largely abandoned.

Akhenaton, his wife Nefertiti and their three daughters are shown in a candid pose in this bas-relief.

....

Jewelry Fashioned From Gold

The jewelry fashioned by goldsmiths for both men and women are among the most beautiful and original ancient Egyptian artifacts. Magnificent masks of gold were placed over the face of the king's mummy. Bejeweled wide collars, bracelets, rings,

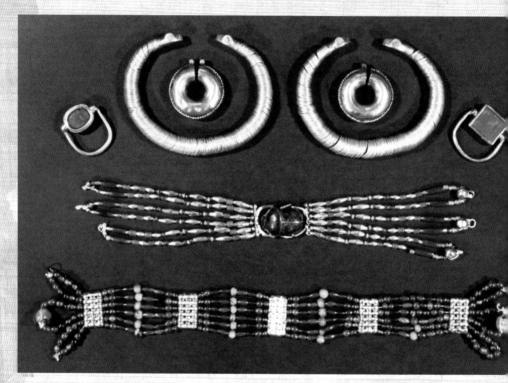

A collection of ancient Egyptian jewelry. In the center of the middle item is a carving of a sacred scarab beetle.

necklaces, earrings, and anklets have been recovered from the tombs. The jewelry is mostly made of gold, but some is silver, which was much scarcer in Egypt, and others are a mixture of gold and silver called electrum. Gems including carnelian, amethyst, lapis lazuli, turquoise, and jasper were often set into, the goldwork.[8]

Calendar

The calendar year, based on the daily appearance of the sun, was a major contribution to civilization from the Old Kingdom. The Egyptians divided the calendar year into twelve months of thirty days each. At the end of each year, five days were added. Each day was divided into twenty-four hours.[9] Today, a modified version of this calendar year is used throughout the world.

Ancient Egypt's hieroglyphs were used from approximately 3100 B.C. to A.D. 400, making them one of the world's oldest writing systems. This hieroglyphic writing includes pictures of a bird, a fish, and musical instruments.

Egyptian Hieroglyphs

Hieroglyphs are a type of picture writing. A picture of a duck can mean "duck," or it could also mean "son." To make clear its meaning, other pictures or signs were added. For example, if the picture was meant to depict a duck, a bird hieroglyph was added to the duck hieroglyph.[10]

Writing for everyday use, known as hieratic, evolved in the Old Kingdom.[11] Hieratic writing consisted of cursive hieroglyphs. The abbreviated pictures or groups of strokes and dots looked very different from the original hieroglyphs. By the seventh century B.C., a third form of writing came into everyday use. It was a shortened version of hieratic known as demotic.

Since all forms of Egyptian writing omitted the use of signs to designate vowels, scholars have not determine with certainty what the written language of the ancient Egyptian sounded like when spoken.[12]

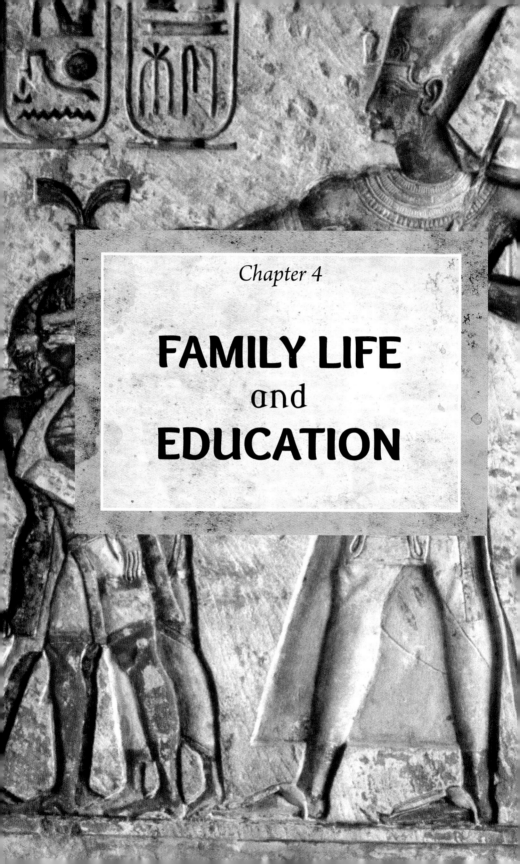

Chapter 4

FAMILY LIFE
and
EDUCATION

Men, women, and children of ancient Egypt lived in close-knit families. Paintings and other artwork depict husbands and wives with their children demonstrating affection for each other and in various family scenes. Most men had one wife, although kings and nobles sometimes had more than one wife.[1]

Marriage contracts provided for the wife's rights, particularly with regard to her property. Women had the right to dispose of their own property. Divorce by either the wife or husband was permitted. In the event of divorce, the wife's property was returned to her, and fathers were made to support their children.[2]

Egyptians valued order and balance in the universe and everyday life. In their temples and homes, they made daily offerings of food and drink to their gods to achieve that order.[3]

Education

Children remained at home with their mothers until age four. Then, fathers began to educate their sons, and mothers began to teach their daughters. Farmers' children received little or no formal education. Boys learned farming skills and crafts of their fathers; girls learned the domestic skills of their mothers, particularly weaving. Above all, children in ancient Egypt were taught to honor their mothers.[4]

Most formal education was limited to boys of the wealthier classes. Most of them attended boarding schools, where they remained until age sixteen. Boys who were intended for the priesthood or government service then went on to further study at temples or in government agencies.[5]

Reading and writing were basic in the schools administered by the government and the temples. The students learned by memorizing texts and then recording what they had memorized. Some students learned how to write letters and prepare documents by copying examples of these.[6] Studies also included ethics, a system of moral values, mathematics, athletics, and manners.[7]

Balls, models of crocodiles with movable jaws, and dolls (some of whose parts were moved by string) were among the typical toys of Egyptian children.[8] Ball games played by both children and adults were popular as were other outdoor activities.

Shelter

Houses in ancient Egypt ranged from the one-room mud hut of the poorest farmer to the elaborate brick or stone home of the wealthy to the king's great palace complex.

Houses generally were made of mud from the Nile baked into bricks or simply dried in the sun. A house might be a single room or a series of rooms built around one or more courtyards. The windows were covered with mats woven from papyrus reeds. Most houses had a flat roof on which the family slept at night.[9]

Food

Bread was the staple food of the ancient Egyptians. It was made from wheat or barley flour and was ground in mortars with pestles or between two stones.[10] Geese and ducks grilled on a spit or roasted over a low hearth formed an important part of the Egyptian diet for wealthier families. The ancient Egyptians also ate fish, but in some districts, it was forbidden because the fish was considered holy or taboo. Beef, lamb, and goat could also be a part of the diet for the wealthy. Vegetables and herbs eaten by ancient Egyptians included onions, lentils, lettuces,

Mud-brick homes overlook a river in Egypt today. These homes are much like those built by ancient Egyptians.

A farmer harvests grain. Bread made from wheat flour or beer made from barley were parts of the Egyptian diet.

garlic, and cucumbers. Fruits such as figs, dates, and grapes were grown throughout Egypt, and honey was used as a sweetener.

Clothing

For most of the people in the working classes of ancient Egypt, clothing was very simple. Egyptian clothing was created to keep cool while in the hot desert. Men wore linen loincloths or kilts whose lengths could vary. They might wear shirts but usually did not. Women wore straight sleeveless linen dresses that could have one or two shoulder straps. These linen clothes were woven by women who used the fibers of the flax plant to make cloth.

Kings, priests, and other members of the elite class wore more elaborate clothing and

These objects, possibly from a tomb, show men herding cattle. Upper-class Egyptians had a fair amount of meat in their diets. They ate the meat of antelope, oxen, sheep, pigs, and goats.

On the left, men can be seen treading grapes to make wine. On the right, men are picking grapes.

For the people of the working classes of ancient Egypt, clothing was very simple. Men wore linen loincloths or kilts. Women wore straight sleeveless linen dresses with one or two shoulder straps.

had many different costumes for different
ceremonies. The way their hair looked was
also important to the ancient Egyptians,
not only for its appearance but also for
what it meant in terms of social status.
They used henna to dye graying hair and
also wore wigs to hide baldness.

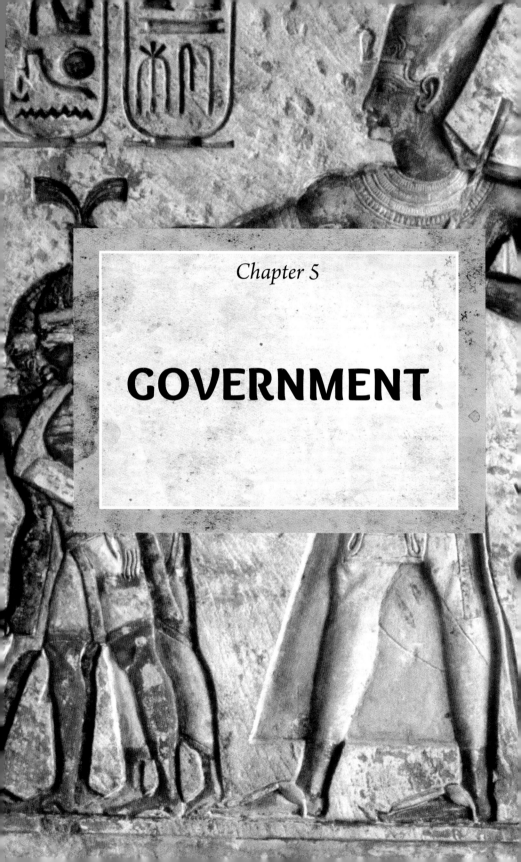

Chapter 5

GOVERNMENT

D espite the changes in dynasties over three thousand years, the original system of government designed by the rulers of the Old Kingdom remained basically unchanged throughout the history of ancient Egypt.[1] The government was so stable and central to Egyptian civilization that it was able to survive internal rebellion from within its borders and attempted takeovers by foreign rulers.

The Pharaoh

In ancient Egypt, the king was absolute ruler, high priest, and military commander in chief. He is frequently shown in battle and always victorious over his enemies, even though some kings died in battle.[2]

The words of the pharaoh when spoken, as written and interpreted by the king's officials, were the only body of law in ancient Egypt.[3] No other codes of law independent of the pharaoh are known to

The Great Temple of Ramses II, located in Nubia. In ancient Egypt, the king was absolute ruler, high priest, and military commander-in-chief. Ramses II, also known as Ramses the Great, is one of Egypt's most famous pharaohs. His sixty-seven-year reign was a time of great prosperity.

have existed. All officials governed in the king's name and only by his authority.

As high priest, the king was believed to be the only human who could comunicate directly with the gods, and therefore was the only one suited to perform certain rites and ceremonies.

Throughout the history of ancient Egypt, there were challenges to the king's authority, especially at times when the king's power was reduced and the central government was weakened or deteriorated completely.

Chief Administrator

The king's chief minister, the tjaty or vizier, handled the daily workings of government in ancient Egypt. It was a very important position, administratively just under the king himself. The chief minister's power extended over a population estimated at about 2 million people in the Old Kingdom and about 3 million people in the New Kingdom.[4]

Government

Under the Old Kingdom, Pepi II appointed a separate minister for Upper and Lower Egypt. As time went on, a large bureaucracy formed that was mostly made up of scribes, men trained in Egyptian forms of writing. Officials were appointed to specialized departments such as the treasury, which collected taxes, and agriculture, which dealt with cultivating the land and harvesting crops.

During periods when the king's authority was not challenged, the government's administrators, acting through the absolute power of the king, were able to organize all of Egypt's resources for the king's enormous construction projects. This was particularly true during the Old Kingdom. Thousands of workers came from all over Egypt to work on the pyramids, tombs, temples, and monuments.[5] This was also likely to happen during periods when farming was not possible, such as during

The Pyramids at Giza. The government's administrators, acting through the absolute power of the king, were able to organize all of Egypt's resources for the king's enormous construction projects. Thousands of workers came from all over Egypt to work on the pyramids.

the flooding of the Nile. In addition to the materials needed for the projects, enormous resources of food, clothing, and other materials were required for the workers and their families.

Nomes, Nomarchs, and Priests

Nomarchs, appointed by the king of Egypt, administered the districts called nomes into which Egypt was divided. Over the years, the office of nomarch became an inherited office. At times, the nomarchs became powerful enough to challenge the king and central government.[6]

The priests of Egypt, under the authority of the king, also helped oversee the government. They supervised the great temple estates located throughout Egypt, each with large numbers of workers, and directed the storage and distribution of the harvests.

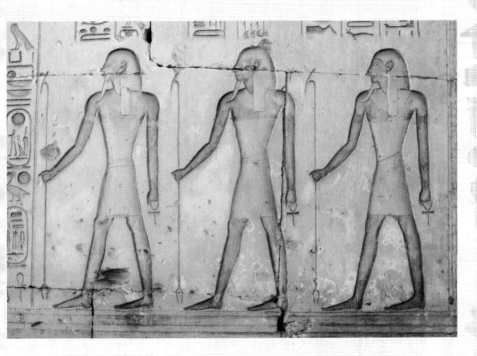

A trio of ancient Egyptian priests carved and painted on the side of a wall of the Temple of Ramses at Abydos, Egypt.

Money and Taxes

Except for the use of gold, some silver, and other metals such as copper and bronze, whose value was determined by weight, there was no money in ancient Egypt.[7] Payment for work on the huge building projects was in the form of rations and goods distributed by the government. Buying and selling between ordinary individuals and traders was mainly by barter. A jar of fat and lumps of metal might be exchanged for an ox.[8]

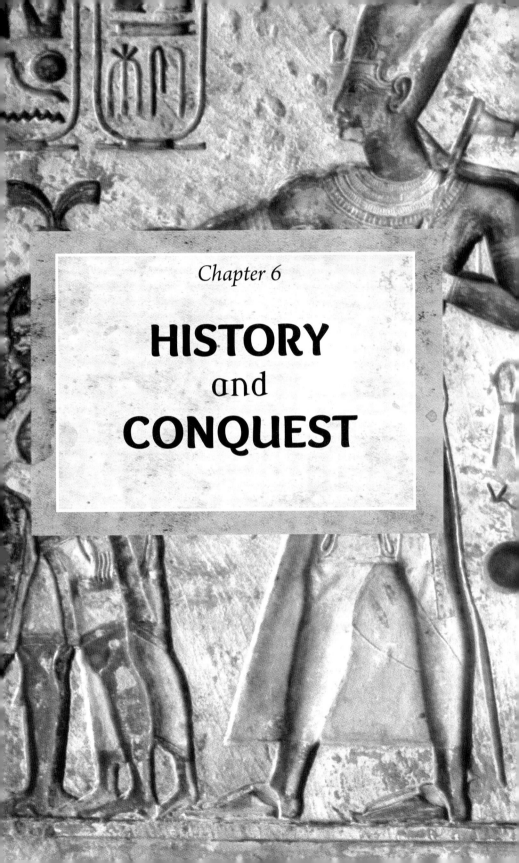

Chapter 6

HISTORY
and
CONQUEST

The kings of the first two dynasties of the Old Kingdom established the basic form of central government rule by an absolute king that lasted throughout the history of ancient Egypt. "Pharaoh" meaning "king," came into use in the late New Kingdom. Before that, it referred to the "great house" of the king.[1]

Menes, the first king of Egypt, unified Upper and Lower Egypt. Unification came about through domination of Lower Egypt by Upper Egypt.[2] Upon unification, Memphis became the capital city for all of Egypt. Memphis remained one of the capital cities throughout the rest of ancient Egypt's history.

King Merenre of the Sixth dynasty sent expeditions into Syria and Palestine. He also expanded Egypt's rule into northern Nubia to the south of the Third Cataract.[3] Otherwise the Old Kingdom remained mostly at peace.

The reign of Pepi II, the last king of the Old Kingdom, lasted from fifty to seventy years. The growth of the number of governors, or nomarchs, during this period was significant.[4]

End of the Old Kingdom

By about 2200 B.C., toward the end of the Old Kingdom, the office of nomarch had become an inherited office, from father to son. This development further weakened the power of the king and central government. Nomarchs divided Egypt between rulers from the city of Thebes and the city of Herakleopolis. Finally, about 1980 B.C., Nebhepetre Mentuhotep II, a king from Thebes, defeated the Herakleopolitan king and Egypt was reunited. A new dynasty established by Amenemhet I, a former minister of Mentuhotep II, began the Middle Kingdom.[5]

The Valley of the Kings contains sixty-two tombs dating from the New Kingdom.

Middle Kingdom

The unity and prosperity of Egypt was
established again under the Middle Kingdom.
Amenemhet II (1818–1772 B.C.) appointed
two ministers—one for Upper Egypt, the
other for Lower Egypt—to administer
the government.

The kings who reigned in the Middle
Kingdom launched expeditions into Libya,
Syria, Palestine, and Nubia.[6] Except for parts
of northern Nubia, Egypt did not annex or
incorporate foreign territory. Instead, it left
troops in the conquered areas to secure
Egypt's borders against invaders. In addition,
these garrisons protected trade routes and
access to resources in the areas.

Second Intermediate Period:

During the Second Intermediate Period, the
Hyksos invaded Egypt and formed the 15th
A small number of Asiatic tribes known as

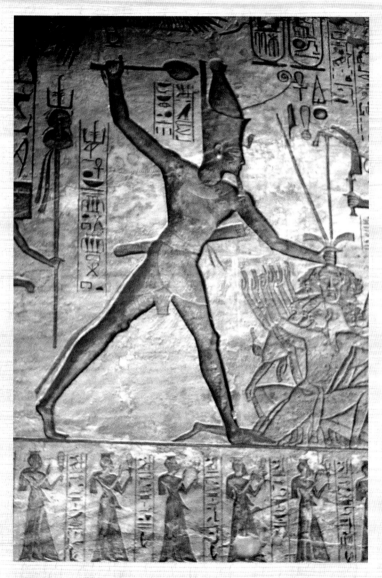

This limestone relief is in the Temple Of Abu Simbel, Egypt. It depicts Ramses II, one of Egypt's most famous pharaoh. As a god-king, he is shown larger than his enemies.

the Hyksos brought about the end of the Middle Kingdom. The Hyksos, who had settled in the Delta, gradually gained control of Lower Egypt and became its rulers, possibly with the help of Nubia. These rulers belong to the Fifteenth dynasty.[7]

The Hyksos did not impose their culture or form of government on Egypt. Instead, as did later conquerors of Egypt, they adopted the forms and practices of the Egyptian kings, including their religion and royal titles. The most important contribution the Hyksos made to Egypt was to increase Egypt's military might. The Hyksos introduced the harnessed horse, a two-wheel chariot, body armor, and new weapons.[8]

For a time, an Egyptian king from Thebes continued to rule Lower Egypt, but eventually even the Theban ruler recognized the rule of the Hyksos.[9]

New Kingdom

Kamose, an Egyptian king in Thebes, went to war with the Hyksos, greatly reducing the Hyksos king's power. However, it was his brother Ahmose (1539–1514 B.C.) who defeated and expelled the Hyksos and unified Egypt. Ahmose's son, Thutmose I, was considered the founder of the Eighteenth dynasty under which the New Kingdom began.[10]

Thutmose I returned the capital of Egypt to Memphis, and Thebes became the center of the worship of Amun with the great temple at Karnak. A great new burial ground of royal tombs known as the Valley of the Kings was begun with the burial there of Thutmose II.[11]

Egypt became an imperial power during the New Kingdom. Thutmose III, who ascended to the throne after the death of his stepmother, Hatshepsut, became

Thutmose III

Egypt's greatest military ruler. He extended Egypt's southern border to the Fourth Cataract in Nubia and conquered Gaza, Palestine, and Syria. Peace between Egypt and the Mitanni Empire (Syria) was finally established when both were threatened by a new power, the Hittites.

Hittites

By 1328 B.C., the Hittites, originally from Anatolia (now Turkey), had conquered most of Syria.[12] The Hittite king had become so powerful that Tutankhamen's widow, Ankhesenamun, asked to marry one of his sons. That son would have become king of Egypt if he had not been murdered on his arrival.

About 1275 or 1274 B.C., Ramses II of the Nineteenth dynasty met the Hittites in a great battle at Kadesh. The temple walls of Ramses II boast of a great victory, but in reality there was no decisive victory. As a result, Egypt and the Hittites remained independent of each other. In 1269 B.C., Egypt, threatened in the west by Libyan forces and the Hittites and in the east by the Assyrians, entered into a peace treaty with the Hittites. Later, marriages between the two kings' families reinforced the treaty.[13]

Ramses II was succeeded by a series of kings who also were named Ramses. These kings and their governments became progressively weaker. Upon the death of Ramses XI, rule of Egypt was divided between rulers in Tanis, a city on a branch of the Nile, and the Amun priesthood in Thebes.[14]

The Third Intermediate Period

The Third Intermediate Period lasted more than four hundred years and was a time of divided rule in Egypt. Libyans, Nubians, and Assyrians succeeded each other in ruling all or parts of Egypt.[15]

Foreign rule produced a notable change in the king's role in religion. In this period, the priests in Thebes increasingly took over the role of the pharaoh in temple ceremonies, and women became prominent in certain sectors of religion. The temple services became more focused on the daughter of the king or high priest as the "god's wife."[16] For the most part, however, the foreign rulers adopted the titles and ceremonies of the pharaoh in Egypt, and life among the ordinary Egyptians continued as it had for centuries.

Late Period

By 656 B.C., Egyptian Prince Psamtek (664–610 B.C.) from the city of Sais in the Delta had ended Assyrian domination and reunited Egypt.[17] In the Late Period, there appears to have been extensive trading with the Greek city-states, and the Egyptians again advanced to the Euphrates River for a brief time. Wars were conducted with Nubia, Libya, and a new power, the Chaldaeans, in the east. However, the greatest threat to Egypt appeared in the form of the new and expanding Persian Empire.

Persian Conquerors

Egypt's independence ended in 525 B.C., with its conquest by Cambyses, king of Persia and son of Cyrus the Great, creator of the Persian Empire. Egypt was made a province of the Persian Empire.

Cambyses took the role and title of pharaoh, kept the Egyptian form of government in place, and honored the Egyptians' gods. His successor, Darius I, continued the practice, restoring temples and monuments and increasing the revenue of the temples.[18]

In 404 B.C., Amyrtaios, an Egyptian, declared himself king and rebelled against Persia. Under Amyrtaios, the Egyptians maintained their independence from 404 B.C.

This mosaic depicts the battle of Alexander the Great against Darius III possibly at Battle of Issus. Alexander, horseman on the left, leads his army against Darius III's Persian forces.

to 343 B.C., when Artaxerxes III, the Persian king, overcame them. However, Persia's rule of Egypt was then threatened by a new power, the Greeks, led by Alexander the Great, king of Macedonia.

Alexander the Great

In 332 B.C., Alexander the Great, after conquering the Persian Empire, invaded and conquered Egypt. There was no great battle; the Egyptians greeted Alexander as a liberator. The Theban priests recognized Alexander as the new ruler of Egypt and named him pharaoh, with the double crown of Upper and Lower Egypt. Alexander accepted with sincere belief in the traditions and religious role of the pharaoh, making sacrifices to the Egyptian gods and restoring the temples at Karnak and Luxor.[19]

Alexander's greatest achievement in Egypt was the founding of a new capital city, Alexandria, on the Mediterranean Sea.

The rear exterior wall of the temple of Dendera carries a huge relief of the queen Cleopatra and Caesarion, her son by Roman leader Julius Caesar. Cleopatra's suicide marked the end of Egypt's self-government.

Alexandria would become one of the richest and most important cities of the ancient world.

In 323 B.C., Alexander died, and his generals then carved up his empire. One of these generals, Ptolemy I, took Egypt as his kingdom. Ptolemy's successors ruled Egypt until the suicide of Cleopatra in 30 B.C., when Egypt became the personal property of the Roman emperor.[20]

TIMELINE

?—3100 B.C. Earliest known communities in ancient Egypt established.

c.3100-2682 B.C. Early Dynastic/Archaic

Upper and Lower Egypt are united. First Egyptian dynasty—rule by members of the same family—established by King Menes.

c.2686-2181 B.C. Old Kingdom

Construction of the pyramids begins.

c.2180-2040 B.C. First Intermediate Period

Political chaos is the norm.

c.2040-1730 B.C. Middle Kingdom

Stability recovered.

c.1730-1550 B.C. Second Intermediate Period

Invasion of Hykos.

c.1550-1080 B.C. New Kingdom

Egyptian Empire created and Akhenaton's religious strategy is begun. Reigns of Thutmose I, II, III, and IV; Hatshepsut; Tutankhamen; and Nefertiti.

c.1080-664 B.C.

Third Intermediate Period

Divided rule by Libyans, Nubians, and Assyrians in succession

c.664-332 B.C.

Late Period

The late Period is divided by some into the Saite Period (664-525 B.C.), when a king from the city of Sias in the Delta ruled a unified Egypt, and the Late Period (525-332 B.C.), when the Persian Empire ruled Egypt. Greek rule began with Alexander the Great, in 332 B.C.

GLOSSARY

A.D.—An abbreviation for the Latin anno Domini, meaning "in the year of our Lord." Used for a measurement of time, A.D. indicates the number of years since the supposed birth date of Christ.

bas-relief—a form of sculpture in which the carved figures are but partly raised from the surface of the stone.

B.C.—Before Christ. Used for a measurement of time, B.C. indicates the number of years before the supposed birth date of Christ.

civilization—A kind of culture marked by a high level of organization in government and religion. Trade, writing, and art are all part of civilization.

culture—A people's way of life.

delta—A deposit of soil that collects at the mouth of a river.

dynasty—A series of rulers who belong to the same family.

empire—A nation and the countries it rules.

hieroglyphics—A type of picture writing used in ancient Egypt.

irrigation—A method of bringing water to a field to foster plant growth

mummy—A body treated for burial with preservatives, to keep it from decaying.

oasis—A place in the desert where trees, shrubs, and other plants can grow because there is water. Plural is *oases*.

papyrus—A plant from which a type of paper was made in ancient Egypt.

pharaoh—An ancient Egyptian ruler.

pyramid—A stone structure that was built as a tomb for the pharaohs of ancient Egypt.

regent—one who governs until a child becomes old enough to rule.

scribe—A person who wrote down things for other people.

vizier—The most important government job in ancient Egypt. The vizier made sure that the pharaoh's orders were carried out.

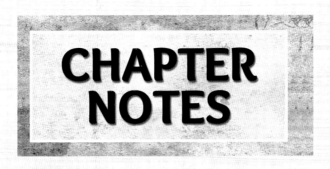

CHAPTER NOTES

Chapter 1. HATSHEPSUT–KING OF EGYPT

1. Joyce Tyldesley, *Hatchepsut, The Female Pharaoh* (New York: Penquin Books USA, Inc., 1996), p. 99.
2. Gay Robins, *Women In Ancient Egypt* (Cambridge, Mass.: Harvard University Press, 1993), p. 51.
3. Barbara Watterson, *Women in Ancient Egypt* (Gloucestershire, Great Britain: Sutton Publishing Limited, 1991), p. 140.
4. Tyldesley, p. 143.
5. Ibid., pp. 145–146.
6. Ian Shaw, *The Oxford History of Ancient Egypt* (New York: Oxford University Press, Inc., 2000), p. 243.
7. Ibid., p. 243.

Chapter 2. LAND, PEOPLE, AND RELIGION

1. Amélie Kuhrt, *The Ancient Near East, c.3000–330 B.C.* (New York: Routledge, 1995), p. 118.
2. Chester G. Starr, *A History of the Ancient World* (New York: Oxford University Press, 1971), p. 55.
3. Kuhrt, p. 124.
4. Starr, p. 53.
5. Kuhrt, p. 120.
6. Barry J. Kemp, *Ancient Egypt, Anatomy of a Civilization* (New York: Routledge, 1991), p. 10.
7. Adolf Erman, *Life in Ancient Egypt* (New York: Dover Publications, Inc., 1971), p. 448.
8. Ibid., p. 447.
9. Pierre Montet, *Eternal Egypt* (New York: The New American Library of World Literature, Inc.. 1964), p. 21.
10. Ibid., pp. 96–97.
11. David P. Silverman, ed., *Ancient Egypt* (New York: Oxford University Press, 1997), p. 86.
12. Ibid., p. 162.
13. Erman, p. 307.
14. Ibid., p. 272.

15. Esmond Wright, ed., *History of the World* (Middlesex, Great Britain: Newnes Books, a division of The Hamlyn Publishing Group Limited, 1985), p. 57.

16. Nicholas Grimal, translated by Ian Shaw, *A History of Ancient Egypt* (Oxford, Great Britain: Blackwell Publishers, 1992), p. 241.

17. Silverman, p. 152.

Chapter 3. ARTS AND CULTURAL CONTRIBUTIONS

1. Claudio Barocas, *Egypt* (New York: Grosset & Dunlap, 1972), p. 24.
2. Sir Alan Gardiner, *The Egyptians, An Introduction* (London: The Folio Society—Oxford University Press, 1961), p. 69.
3. Barocas, p. 27.
4. Chester G. Starr, *A History of the Ancient World* (New York: Oxford University Press, 1971), p. 58.
5. Sir J. Gardner Wilkinson, *The Ancient Egyptians, Their Life and Gods, Vol. I* (London: Studio Editions, Ltd., 1990), pp. 86–87.
6. Irmgard Woldering, *The Art of Egypt, The Time of the Pharoahs* (New York: Greystone Press, 1965), p. 95.
7. Ibid., p. 170.
8. Barbara Watterson, *Women in Ancient Egypt* (Gloucestershire, Great Britain: Sutton Publishing Limited, 1991), pp. 106–107.
9. Starr, p. 62.
10. Nicholas Grimal, translated by Ian Shaw, *A History of Ancient Egypt* (Oxford, Great Britain: Blackwell Publishers, 1992), p. 33.
11. Adolf Erman, *Life in Ancient Egypt* (New York: Dover Publications, Inc., 1971), p. 339.
12. Jacquetta Hawkes, *The First Great Civilizations: Life in Mesopotamia, the Indus Valley, and Egypt* (New York: Alfred A. Knopf, 1977), p. 438.

Chapter 4. FAMILY LIFE AND EDUCATION

1. Adolf Erman, *Life in Ancient Egypt* (New York: Dover Publications, Inc., 1971), p. 151.
2. Esmond Wright, ed., *History of the World* (Middlesex, Great Britain: Newnes Books, a division of The Hamlyn Publishing Group Limited, 1985), p. 87.
3. David P. Silverman, ed., *Ancient Egypt* (New York: Oxford University Press, 1997), p. 148.
4. Erman, p. 155.
5. Barbara Watterson, *Women in Ancient Egypt* (Gloucestershire, Great Britain: Sutton Publishing Limited, 1991), p. 124.
6. Wright, p. 88.
7. Erman, p. 165.
8. Sir J. Gardner Wilkinson, *The Ancient Egyptians, Their Life and Gods, Vol. I* (London: Studio Editions, Ltd., 1990), pp. 196–197.
9. Ibid., p. 7.
10. Erman, p. 189.

Chapter Notes

Chapter 5. GOVERNMENT

1. Nicholas Grimal, translated by Ian Shaw, *A History of Ancient Egypt* (Oxford, Great Britain: Blackwell Publishers, 1992), p. 93.
2. David P. Silverman, ed., *Ancient Egypt* (New York: Oxford University Press, 1977), pp. 108–109.
3. Grimal, p. 58.
4. Esmond Wright, ed., *History of the World* (Middlesex, Great Britain: Newnes Books, a division of The Hamlyn Publishing Group Limited, 1985), p. 94.
5. Silverman, p. 67.
6. Ibid., p. 27.
7. Barry J. Kemp, *Ancient Egypt, Anatomy of a Civilization* (New York: Routledge, 1991), p. 117.
8. Ibid., p. 248.

Chapter 6. HISTORY AND CONQUEST

1. David P. Silverman, ed., *Ancient Egypt* (New York: Oxford University Press, 1997), p. 109.
2. Nicholas Grimal, translated by Ian Shaw, *A History of Ancient Egypt* (Oxford, Great Britain: Blackwell Publishers, 1992), p. 48.
3. Ibid., p. 87.
4. Silverman, p. 26.
5. Ibid., p. 27.
6. Grimal, p. 155.
7. Ibid., pp. 185–186.
8. Joyce Tyldesley, *Hatchepsut, The Female Pharaoh* (New York: Penquin Books USA, Inc., 1996), p. 21.
9. Silverman, p. 31.
10. Grimal, pp. 192–193.
11. Kuhrt, p. 191.
12. O.R. Gurney, *The Hittites* (London: The Folio Society—Penquin Books Inc., 1990), p. 28.
13. Kuhrt, p. 207.
14. Ibid., p. 210.
15. Ibid., p. 623.
16. Ian Shaw, *The Oxford History of Ancient Egypt* (New York: Oxford University Press Inc., 2000), pp. 359–360.
17. Ibid., p. 371.
18. Jacquetta Hawkes, *The First Great Civilizations: Life in Mesopotamia, the Indus Valley, and Egypt* (New York: Alfred A. Knopf, 1977), p. 321.
19. Peter Green, *Alexander of Macedon 356–323 B.C.* (Berkeley and Los Angeles: University of California Press, 1991), pp. 269–270.
20. Grimal, pp. 2–3.
21. Ardagh, Philip. *Ancient Egypt.* Columbus, Ohio: McGraw-Hill Children's Publishing, 2000.

FURTHER READING

BOOKS

Challen, Paul. *Life in Ancient Egypt*. New York: Crabtree Publishing Co., 2005.

Harris, Geraldine. *Ancient Egypt*. New York: Chelsea House, 2007.

Hinds, Kathryn. *Religion*. New York: Marshall Cavendish Benchmark, 2007.

Kallen, Stuart A. *Ancient Egypt*. San Diego, CA: Reference Point Press, 2012.

Kennett, David. *Pharaoh: Life and Afterlife of a God*. New York: Walker & Co., 2012.

Meltzer, Milton. *In the Days of the Pharaohs: A Look at Ancient Egypt*. New York: Franklin Watts, 2001.

Pemberton, Delia. *Atlas of Ancient Egypt*. New York: Harry N. Abrams, in association with the British Museum, 2005.

Weitzman, David. *Pharaoh's Boat*. Boston: Houghton Mifflin Harcourt, 2009.

INTERNET ADDRESSES

The British Museum: Ancient Egypt

Explore the British Museum's resources on Egyptian history, life, geography, religion, and customs.

<www.ancientegypt.co.uk>

KIDPEDE: Ancient Egypt for Kids–Homework Help for Ancient Egypt

<www.historyforkids.org/learn/egypt>

NOVA: Explore Ancient Egypt–PBS: Public Broadcasting Service

<www.pbs.org/wgbh/nova/ancient/ explore-ancient-egypt.htm>

INDEX

Index